Chuck Swindoll overlooking the Old City of Jerusalem

Up to *Jerusalem*

SOME PLACES *are so* SIGNIFICANT that when we visit them they seem almost sacred. Jerusalem is like that. The streets and hills of this timeless city have a history to tell us, if we will but visit their scenes carefully and, might I add, slowly. That's what these next pages are intended to do: to lead you day by day through the most epochal week in history by revisiting the places where the Son of God spent His final days on earth.

As you trace the events of Christ's Passion Week in Jerusalem, I invite you to fully engage, not just with a place but with a Person. Meet Jesus with new eyes. See again (or for the first time) the One whose violent sufferings and crushing death wrought a wondrous saving work—a springtide of mercy and grace to the whole world.

It's important that we linger over the truths of Scripture . . . to sense the pain . . . to observe the reproach . . . to marvel at the cost . . . to explore the wonder of how that which was separated by an abyss of wrong was reconciled by the deed of perfect love.

Every time I come to the week before Easter, I mentally revisit Jerusalem. I travel with Jesus as He leaves a distant place—the other side of the Jordan River—and makes His way through the hot desert region toward Jericho, across the Wadi Qilt, and then up to *Yerushalaim*.

Look for Him now in your mind's eye, coming to Jerusalem, focused on the purpose that overshadowed His entire life. For the joy set before Him, Jesus walked on to the Holy City.

Picture yourself back in time, perched on the edge of the week on which all of history still turns. Now, day by day, catch a glimpse of the geography and ponder the story behind each scene from Scripture. Experience the Passion Week like never before—in the place where it actually happened.

In the pages of *Sunday to Sunday: A Pictorial Journey Through the Passion Week*, we invite you to remember the greatest act of love and grace that history has ever known. It will empower you to worship Him who died for you and exalt Him who was raised for you. Why? So you might live a transformed life.

I invite you to come with me now as we walk through history. Let's visit the places and experience the events from that Passion Week in April almost two thousand years ago. Let's follow the Lord Jesus Christ, whose courageous determination and discipline to stay with the obedient path led ultimately to a cross . . . and then to His great and glorious resurrection from the grave.

Make sure you pause and let the wonder sink in.

Hosanna! He is risen! He is risen indeed!

In Christ, our Messiah and Savior,

Chuck

Charles R. Swindoll

Valley of Jehoshaphat

Mount of Olives

Herod's Gate

Stephen's Gate (Sheep Gate)

Garden of Gethsemane

Damascus Gate

Antonio Fortress

Church of the Holy Sepulcher

Where the Temple Stood

Eastern Gate

Kidron Valley

Temple Mount

Jaffa Gate

Western Wall

Citadel

Dung Gate

City of David

Zion Gate

Church of St. Peter in Gallicantu

Field of Blood

Mount Zion

Hinnom Valley

The Old City of Jerusalem (all gates have modern names).

Itinerary

UP TO JERUSALEM 1

KEY LOCATIONS IN THE PASSION WEEK. 2

PALM SUNDAY 4

MONDAY 12

TUESDAY 20

WEDNESDAY. 28

THURSDAY 36

FRIDAY. 46

SATURDAY 58

EASTER SUNDAY. 62

HOW TO BEGIN A RELATIONSHIP WITH GOD 70

WE ARE HERE FOR YOU. 72

ORDERING INFORMATION. 72

ENDNOTES. 73

PALM
Sunday

View of the Temple Mount from the Mount of Olives

Just over the hill from Jerusalem, Bethany—the hometown of Jesus's friends Lazarus, Martha, and Mary—was likely Jesus's home base while in Jerusalem.

BEHOLD, *your king is coming* TO YOU;

HE IS JUST AND ENDOWED WITH SALVATION,

humble, AND MOUNTED ON A *donkey.*

— ZECHARIAH 9:9

Every year of *His* life, Jesus journeyed to Jerusalem for the Passover. Every turn in the road was as familiar to Him as a trip home.

Until this year Jesus had resisted the limelight and had refused to make a name for Himself. Never had He carried a big sign or choreographed an entrance. But today was different.

Jesus borrowed a young donkey and rode down the Mount of Olives, in fulfillment of Scripture.

For the first and only time, on this Sunday, Jesus accepted the praises of the general public. He asked for a donkey to ride, fulfilling the prophet Zechariah's five-hundred-year-old prediction that the King would come, humble and mounted on a colt. Jesus knew full well the statement He was making. He was revealing Himself as the Messiah, the long-awaited King of Israel.

So He let the crowd wave palm branches and sing His praises. He let them announce, "Hosanna in the highest!" in fulfillment of Psalm 118:26, "Blessed is the one who comes in the name of the LORD." He let them say it. He let them yell it. It was almost a mob scene.

Yet somewhere along the road, Jesus was surely struck with the reality of their imminent change of heart. He had come to save them, answering their cries, "Hosanna—*save us now!*" but He knew the next few days would finalize their rejection of Him as Messiah. And on Friday they would slam the door on His offer of salvation.

Jesus knew exactly what day it was.

The prophet Daniel had penned a meticulous prediction of the exact day when the Messiah would appear in Jerusalem. Exactly 483 Jewish calendar years from the rebuilding of Jerusalem in March 444 BC, "Messiah the Prince" would appear (Daniel 9:25).[1] If the Jewish leaders had taken seriously Daniel's challenge to "know and discern" the timing, Jesus would have topped the hill on this day to see a "Welcome, Messiah!" banner draped over the walls of Jerusalem. Instead, the Jewish leaders rebuked the notion that the people so easily embraced. They wanted no part of Jesus as the "Son of David." They wanted a king like all the other nations had.

It hardly seemed a "triumphal entry" at all.[2]

See Psalm 118:25–26; Daniel 9:25; Zechariah 9:9–10; and Matthew 21:1–9.

Days before, Mary of Bethany broke open an alabaster jar, perhaps like this one, and anointed Jesus for burial with precious oil, an insightful acknowledgement of Jesus's upcoming messianic sacrifice.

A panoramic view of the Old City of Jerusalem through the window of the Church of Dominus Flevit—which means, "the Lord wept"

WHEN HE APPROACHED JERUSALEM,
HE *saw* THE CITY
AND *wept* OVER IT.
—LUKE 19:41

CRIPTURE RECORDS THAT *Jesus* cried twice in the weeks leading up to the cross. The first was in Bethany, just over the hill from Jerusalem, when He stood with close friends Martha and Mary at their brother Lazarus's tomb.

Of this occasion, John 11:35 records simply, "Jesus wept." We stand as silent witnesses to this private moment in Jesus's life. The word for weeping here is used only once in the Bible; it means "to shed tears."[3] It's a quiet word describing the quiet tears that stream down someone's face when lost in grief. The more common word for weeping was used to indicate "any loud expression of grief . . . wailing."[4] John 11:33 says that Mary wept loudly like this as she stood there beside Jesus. But Jesus's tears held a different emotion.

Jesus also cried on Palm Sunday as He made His messianic entrance into Jerusalem—just five days before He would face death. But this time, His tears weren't quiet. Luke 19:41 says He wailed, just as Mary had done at Lazarus's tomb.

Did He cry because He knew the final countdown to the cross had begun? No, this thought wasn't new to Jesus. He had lived each moment in the shadow

This sculptured relief in Dominus Flevit depicts Jesus weeping as He entered Jerusalem.

of a sure and certain appointment declared before the foundation of the world. Just days earlier, He had told His disciples He was going to die in Jerusalem.

Why, then, did He cry? Jesus wept because He knew what lay ahead for Jerusalem, the city He loved. He wept for the people, whom He loved even more. He cried because He knew how they searched for salvation everywhere except where they could find it. He cried at their loud "Hosannas" because He knew they missed the point. The people shouted, "Blessed is He who comes in the name of the Lord; Hosanna in the highest!" Their words echoed Psalm 118:25–26 as they sought political freedom and prosperity from the Messiah. They expected God's kingdom immediately, although Jesus had taught them otherwise. They celebrated Him as the soon-to-be king but rejected Him as their Savior. Perhaps the gripping reality of their rejection and all it would mean to their future sank in as He gazed at the city.

At the moment you'd think He would cry for Himself, Jesus wept for the sheep He had come to save—yet they ran from His rescue.

See Luke 13:34–35; 19:41–44; 23:28–31; and John 11:35.

The Dominus Flevit dome, shaped in the form of an inverted teardrop

On His triumphal entry, Jesus entered Jerusalem through the Eastern Gate, perhaps located near Stephen's Gate of today.

WHEN HE HAD ENTERED *Jerusalem*,
ALL THE CITY WAS *stirred*, SAYING,
"WHO IS THIS?"

— MATTHEW 21:10

WHO DO PEOPLE SAY THAT *I am?*

Jesus had asked His disciples that question before.

It was a good question—one that very few got right.

To the soldiers guarding the Temple Mount, Jesus was a rebel, a renegade wannabe king guilty of treason. To the Jewish leaders mingling in the crowd, Jesus was a threat, a blasphemer with divine delusions, and worthy of death. And to the Jewish crowds, excited but confused, Jesus was their deliverer—from oppression, from Rome, and from all things political.

They missed the truth. But a few got it right.

- Such as the children who called Jesus "the Son of David."

- Or Andrew. Staggering and out of breath, he was the first to say, "We have found Him . . . we have found the Messiah."

- John the Baptist pointed to Jesus and said, "Behold, the Lamb of God!"

- And Martha, Jesus's good friend, confessed, "Yes, Lord; I have believed that You are the Christ, the Son of God, even He who comes into the world."

The important question today is: Who do you say Jesus is? A good man? A respected teacher? One among many wise philosophers?

Just so you're aware, you *will* answer that question one day. Some may hope to dodge it, but the day is racing toward you when your only answer must be, as Peter's was, Jesus is "the Christ, the Son of the living God." Will you say now, "You are the One and Only! My Savior! The Messiah!"

Upon this declaration you will discover that:

- No one else is qualified to grant forgiveness of your sin but the One, Jesus.

- No one else will stay as close to you as Christ when all else is stripped away.

- No one else can satisfy your greatest need—your need for a Savior.

And that's just in this life. When you've taken your last breath and stepped into eternity, Jesus alone is qualified to escort you from the grave to glory.

All this and an eternity with God are the result of what you confess about Jesus. Your destiny changes with your answer.

See Matthew 16:14–16; John 1:29, 41; 11:27; and Philippians 2:9–11.

As Jesus rode into Jerusalem down the Mount of Olives, people waved palm branches, a symbol of national pride. When they cried, "Hosanna!" they were calling out to Jesus, saying, "Save us!" In essence, they told Him, "Come be our king and rescue us from the Romans."

Monday

Model of the Temple Mount as it appeared in Jesus's day

Seeing a lone *fig tree* by the road, He came to it and found *nothing* on it except leaves only; and He said to it, "*No longer* shall there ever be any *fruit* from you."

— MATTHEW 21:19

The fig tree produced a common treat for the poor and the gleaners in Jesus's day.

JUDGING BY APPEARANCES, *Jerusalem* is surely the most religious place on earth. Pious sects of all varieties color the busy sidewalks. Their unique customs and rules dictate the dress, foods, habits, and values of their members. In this respect, the city hasn't changed much in two millennia.

But Jesus never judged by appearances. On this Monday of His final week, Jesus and the disciples passed by a large, shady fig tree on their way into the city. Jesus was hungry and looked for some fig buds to snack on, a common treat of the day. Yet, in spite of the promising leafy foliage, there were no buds—a sure sign that the tree would bear no fruit later that season. Jesus cursed the tree for being all show but no substance.

1 Pet. 3:18

It wasn't hard to pick up on Jesus's greater heartbreak. All around Him in Jerusalem was an impressive appearance of spirituality, but He knew the hearts of worshippers and ached at their hypocrisy. Religious, yes, but with no heart for God. *Ps. 51:16-17   Hos. 6:6   Ps. 40:6   Heb 10:8-10*

In spite of all the pious trappings of loud prayers and rigorous duty, Israel was barren. Impressive outward appearances of sacred dress and legalistic lifestyles belied the fact that Israel's heart was far from God. In spite of God's outrageous favor, Israel simply bore no fruit. Jesus seemingly saw the parallel in the fig tree and, in His curse, warned of God's impending judgment on Israel. The disciples caught the message and probably felt the hot, haunting wind at their necks when they passed the tree again the next day and found it had dried up and died.

Empty religion fails to impress God—every time.

See 1 Samuel 16:7; Mark 11:12–14, 19–22; and Luke 16:15.

A fig bud

A withered fig tree

An average day at the cotton market in the Arab Quarter of the Old City

For everyone who *does evil* hates the Light,
and does not come to the *Light*
for fear that his *deeds* will be *exposed.*

—JOHN 3:20

I N *most* WAYS, the Jerusalem that Jesus entered on this Monday was very different from the city we experience today. But in some ways, it wasn't.

In no way is this better seen than in the collision between faith and commerce. Money changers shortchanged the pilgrims who came to the temple to worship; merchants sold clean animals that would have dunged up the temple grounds, defiling God's place of worship.

Jesus displayed His authority as Messiah by promptly cleaning house, just as He had done three years earlier. He drove out those who used worship as an opportunity for financial gain—a charade the Lord still despises.

"Is it not written," Jesus reminded them, "'My house shall be called a house of prayer for all the nations'? But you have made it a robbers' den." The phrase "robbers' den" comes from Jeremiah's rebuke to those who abused God's first temple in the prophet's day. Jeremiah had stood in that temple and told the leaders to go to Shiloh to see what remained of the tabernacle. Its ruins foreshadowed the destruction of the first temple. And Jesus, quoting Jeremiah, predicted the same grievous outcome for the second temple.

Words and works like Jesus's on this Monday did little to curry the favor of the Jewish leaders. Instead, they began looking for a way to kill Him. Every day Jesus taught in the temple, and steadily their anger toward Him swelled. Why? Because light reveals what lurks in darkness. In the bright light of truth, Jesus was exposing their hypocrisy.[1]

See Jeremiah 7:11–12; Mark 11:17–18; Luke 19:47; and John 1:5; 2:14–16; 3:19–21; 8:12.

The Jaffa Gate leads to one of the most popular shopping districts in Jerusalem and marks the beginning of the road that descends to the west coast port of Jaffa on the Mediterranean Sea.

The ruins of the tabernacle at Shiloh, referred to by the prophet Jeremiah. "I called you but you did not answer, therefore, I will do to the house which is called by My name, in which you trust, and to the place which I gave you and your fathers, as I did to Shiloh" (Jeremiah 7:13–14).

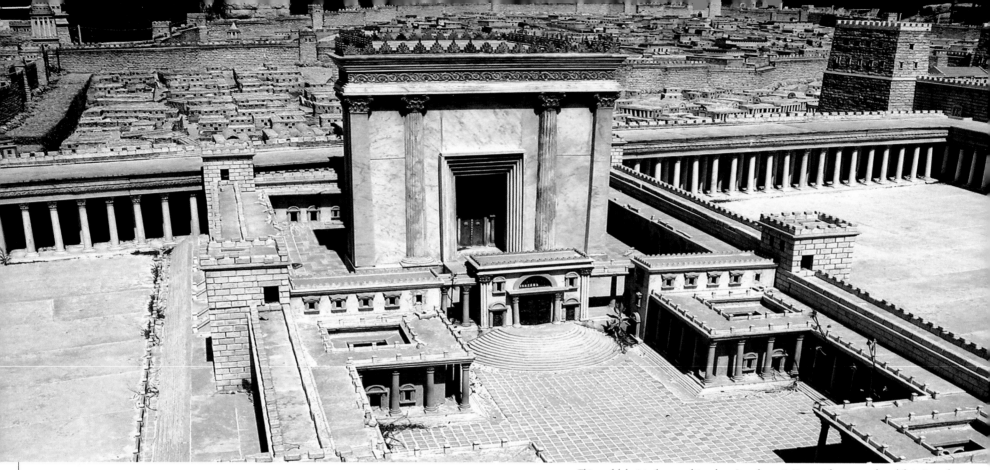

This model depicts the second temple as Jesus knew it. He went there every day while in Jerusalem.

AND ALL THE PEOPLE WOULD GET UP *early* IN THE MORNING
TO *come* TO HIM IN THE TEMPLE
to listen TO HIM.

— LUKE 21:38

ONE WEEK TO *Live*

I f you *knew* that you had just one more week to live, how would you spend it? If on a Monday you knew that by Saturday night your body would be in a box and your soul would have exited the earth, what difference would it make in what you did in the next five days?

This was a question that Jesus had to answer. Like no one else, He knew that this was His last week, and so He spent His time in two areas that He considered to be of paramount importance.

In this final week, Jesus was tethered to the temple. He lingered inside its walls every day, jealous for its purity and protective of what went on in its courts. He spent His final days teaching, defending eternal truth, exposing error, and inspiring faith.

In this final week, Jesus also demonstrated His priority for the ones He loved to the uttermost, His disciples. He wrapped Himself in humility and served them. He washed their feet. He talked and walked with them. He gave them instruction they would need to carry on without Him. He listened and received love from these ones who would feel the immediate sting of His death more than any others.

Jesus lived His final week under the crushing weight that His time had come. His long-anticipated sacrifice was imminent, so these final minutes were precious and few.

The countdown had begun.

See Luke 19:47–48 and John 13:1, 5, 31–35.

Thousands of Jewish graves cover the Mount of Olives. Overlooking the Temple Mount, it was a premium burial location reserved for only the "most religious."

Jesus's final days were spent with people He loved.

Tuesday

Excavations at the southern end of the Temple Mount, with the Mount of Olives in the background

White sepulchers cover the slope of the Mount of Olives. In Jewish tradition, the small rocks placed on the tombs are a symbol of respect for the deceased. Adding one small stone allows mourners unable to attend the funeral to continue in the burial of the person who lies in the tomb.

Jerusalem, JERUSALEM, WHO *kills* THE PROPHETS AND *stones* THOSE WHO ARE SENT TO HER! HOW OFTEN I WANTED TO *gather* YOUR CHILDREN TOGETHER, THE WAY A *hen* GATHERS *her chicks* UNDER HER *wings*, AND YOU WERE *unwilling*.

— MATTHEW 23:37

TEMPLE *Controversy*

T HE *division* BETWEEN JESUS AND THE PHARISEES had never been anything less than a wide canyon. He came to speak truth; they desired control. One fact will always be true of controllers: what they cannot control, they seek to destroy.

The Pharisees anticipated the arrival of a conquering Messiah. Their tradition said He would come suddenly to His temple. Indeed, He had arrived, but not as they had expected.

Jesus forcefully handed down to them what could very well be the sharpest rebuke recorded in Scripture. Eight times He uttered "woe," an exclamation used to express deep, anguished sorrow over something grievous. It is an emphatic denunciation of sin. Seven times He called the scribes and Pharisees "hypocrites." Five times He called them "blind." And in this stinging indictment, Jesus spelled out a detailed catalog of sins that had been plainly evident for years and had gone unchecked. But no more! The true Messiah had come to take His stand for truth in the place where truth was being trampled. How they hated Him across that wide canyon!

The Pharisees would have seized Jesus on the spot were it not for the thousands of people who openly supported Him. He traveled freely around the city and taught regularly in the temple, protected from assassination by His immense popularity. His enemies would have to catch Him alone and unaware. But, for that, they would need help from someone on the inside.[1]

See Matthew 23:13–36.

Stones typical of what mourners leave on graves, signifying, "I was here to honor you."

"TRULY I SAY TO YOU, *not one stone* HERE WILL BE LEFT UPON ANOTHER, WHICH WILL NOT BE *torn down.*"

— MATTHEW 24:2

Recent excavations have uncovered a first-century street dating to before the second temple's destruction in AD 70. The pavement had been literally crushed and pressed into the ground by the massive stones that the Romans had hurled down from the temple onto the street. Excavators uncovered most of the street but left one pile of stones just as they found them. What Jesus predicted had happened.

IT WAS *Tuesday.*

Two days prior, Jesus had entered Jerusalem riding on a donkey, heralded by cries of "Hosanna!"

Two days later, Jesus would be "captured," absurdly tried, tortured, and then sacrificed on the following day to cries of "Crucify Him!"

It was a confusing time.

But not for Jesus. He was as resolute in His mission as ever. He had come to die as a holy payment for humanity's sin—and nothing would stop Him.

The disciples listened to Jesus talk of His upcoming death with puzzled panic. *What?* They had anticipated they would reign alongside this coming King, who had now arrived. They thought they would be the ones who would serve in His kingdom. That's why they left their nets to follow Him. They even left successful law practices and tax businesses. He was the One who would conquer the enemy. But now He said He would be handed over to the enemy. And after they scourged Him, Jesus said, they would kill Him. Then on the third day, Jesus said, He would rise again.

The disciples understood none of these things.

The plan was just not unfolding the way they anticipated. They heard His words, they knew the Word, but they just couldn't piece it together. They knew who He was. Their search was over. They had found the One. But now His words made no sense.

The religious officials were also confused. For three and a half years, Jesus had been a thorn in their side. *Him, Messiah? No way. We will not have this man rule over us!*

From their perspective, Jesus needed to be permanently removed before He incited the people to riot. But today, Tuesday, they pulled back, afraid of the crowds. Jesus's actions on Sunday and Monday had forced them to a point of no return. And the conspiracy kicked into gear—they needed to grab Him before He tried to escape.

But Jesus wouldn't attempt to escape Jerusalem. He courageously placed Himself right in their path. This was His path of obedience.

See Luke 18:31–34; 19:45–48.

This fallen stone from the second temple bears a Hebrew inscription that means: "To the Place of Trumpeting." The stone represented the spot high above the city where Jewish priests would stand and blow a shofar (ram's horn pictured below) to announce the Sabbath and the start of festival days. Some say this represented the pinnacle of the temple. If so, Jesus would have stood beside this stone when Satan tempted Him to jump off. (See Matthew 4:6.)

Late afternoon in Jerusalem, the sun sets over the Old City.

JESUS ANSWERED AND SAID TO THEM, "SEE TO IT THAT NO ONE *misleads* YOU. FOR MANY *will come* IN MY NAME, SAYING, 'I AM THE *Christ,*' AND WILL *mislead* MANY."

— MATTHEW 24:4–5

O N   T H I S   *Tuesday*,   L A T E   I N   T H E   A F T E R N O O N,   the disciples sat with Jesus on the Mount of Olives, overlooking the Old City. The sun hung low in the west, sending a golden cast across the Temple Mount where they had spent most of the day.

Now, looking at the grand architecture from their high vantage point, Jesus's ominous prophecy, made as they left the temple, that "not one stone will be left upon another which will not be torn down," took on new meaning. The news about this sure and frightening future rocked them.

Because the people of Israel would reject Jesus's offer of the kingdom, their house would be destroyed and they would lose the privilege of being God's representatives in the present age.

And especially heartbreaking to the disciples, Jesus had said He was going away and would not return until Israel repented and recognized Him as the legitimate Messiah at the end of the age.

"When will this happen? What will be the sign?" they asked now as they sat with Him.

And from that panoramic vista, Jesus laid out the grim chain of events that would occur in Israel's future before the time when He promised to again stand on this same spot, but then as reigning King.

As a substitute for their requested details, Jesus cautioned them, "See to it that no one misleads you." Jesus knew that when it came to talk about the future, people would believe anything, pay anything, and do anything for a peek behind tomorrow's curtain. He knew future generations would be conned by religious hucksters who would sell tickets to coming attractions without any thought at all to what God had said.

But in spite of that, Jesus called His followers to faithfulness in carrying out His commands, asking them to entrust to God their expectation for things to come and reminding them that He will not forget Israel and will do what He says He will do.

See Matthew 24:3 – 31; Mark 13:3 – 37; Luke 21:5 – 28; and 1 John 2:18.

A Jew praying at the Western Wall

As early as the second century BC and continuing today, Israel's "devout" have worn tefillin, loosely transliterated from Greek as "phylacteries," on their heads. By Jesus's day, the Pharisees' phylacteries had grown so large and conspicuous that Jesus condemned the Pharisees' religious pride. (See Matthew 23:5.)

Wednesday

Southern excavations of the Temple Mount

Every devout Jew longs to be in Jerusalem for Passover. The Passover has become, to a large degree, a traditional celebration, but it was designed by God to be a lasting memorial of His faithfulness to the community of Israel. (See Exodus 12:14.)

JERUSALEM . . . TO WHICH THE TRIBES *go up,* EVEN THE TRIBES OF THE LORD — AN ORDINANCE FOR ISRAEL — TO *give thanks* TO THE NAME OF THE LORD.

—PSALM 122:3–4

To the *Jewish* PEOPLE, NO PLACE IS MORE PRECIOUS than Jerusalem. After the people were taken into captivity in 586 BC, they pronounced an oath beside the streams of Babylon to remember and not forget their beloved Jerusalem. And they never have.

To the devout Jew today, nothing is more sacred in Jerusalem than the Western Wall of the Temple Mount. This wall represents a portion of the original retaining wall upon which the second temple stood. The first temple was destroyed by invading Babylonians in 586 BC. The second temple, built by Zerubbabel and then expanded upon by Herod, was the one Jesus knew. Made of limestone, marble, and gold, Herod's temple was taller than a fifteen-story building. It could accommodate hundreds of thousands of pilgrims at one time and was twice the size of the largest temple enclosure in Rome, clearly the greatest building project of the Roman world in its day. It was destroyed by the Romans in AD 70.

What remains today is the 1,500-foot retaining wall of the Temple Mount that stood closest to the Holy of Holies, where the glory of God, His *shekinah*, dwelled. The section of the wall that is exposed is the place where devout Jews today remember their lost glory and long for a rebuilt temple. When they pray, bobbing in worship, they face the wall so as to get as close as possible to the place where the glory of God once dwelled. Sadly, they stand atop thirty feet of rubble consisting of stones from the destroyed temple they lament.

See 2 Chronicles 3:1–17; Ezra 4:8–13; 5:1–2, 14–18; Psalm137; and Matthew 27:40.

For centuries, people have stuffed tzetels, prayers written on scraps of paper, into the ancient cracks of the Western Wall, called the Kotel. They believe that their requests will find a shortcut to God's ear in this place considered so sacred.

Woman praying at the Western Wall

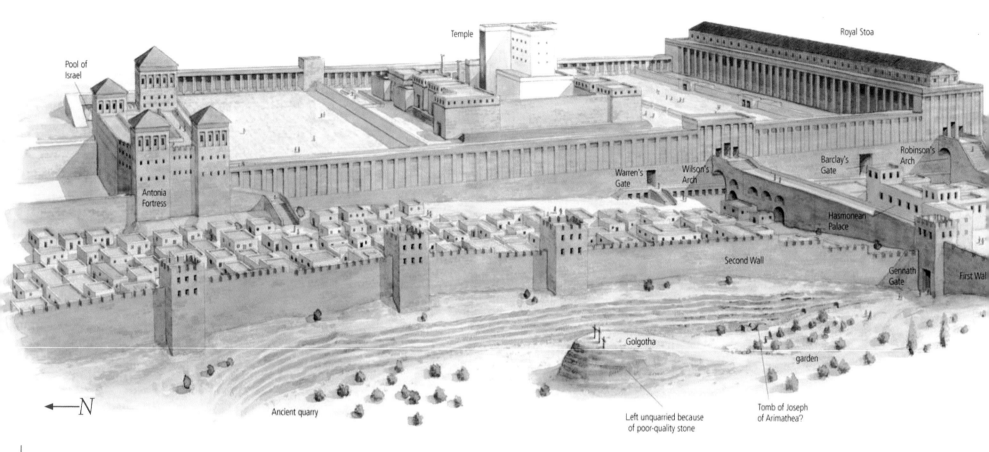

Temple

Royal Stoa

Pool of
Israel

Antonia
Fortress

Warren's
Gate

Wilson's
Arch

Barclay's
Gate

Robinson's
Arch

Hasmonean
Palace

Second Wall

Gennath
Gate

First Wall

←—N

Ancient quarry

Golgotha

garden

Left unquarried because
of poor-quality stone

Tomb of Joseph
of Arimathea?

*This illustration shows what the temple complex and the Old City of Jerusalem would have looked like at the time of Christ.
Notice the proximity of the cross (Golgotha) to the temple, as well as the tomb of Joseph of Arimathea where Jesus was laid.*

IN THE BEGINNING WAS THE *Word*, AND THE WORD *was with God*,
AND THE WORD *was God*. . . . AND THE WORD *became flesh*,
AND *dwelt among us*, AND WE SAW HIS *glory*.

—JOHN 1:1, 14

When the children of Israel wandered in the desert, they worshipped God in the tabernacle. This full-scale model building was created using the God-designed plans in Exodus 26–28.

During Passover, every family offered a sacrificial lamb.

GOD'S PLAN THROUGH *the centuries* has been for His people to draw near to Him as He dwells with them. He has done that first in the tent of a tabernacle, then in an exclusively holy temple room, then on earth in the person of His Son Jesus, and now through His Spirit living in all believers in Christ.

The first temple in Jerusalem, envisioned by David and built by Solomon, was the place where God chose His glory to reside. The beautiful structure became a symbol of God's presence on earth, a place where people could go when they wanted to be near God. That temple was destroyed in 586 BC. Another temple was built some 70 years later by Zerubbabel and expanded upon by Herod the Great to become the magnificent structure of Jesus's day. But by then, God's presence had left the temple because of Israel's disbelief.

In relentless pursuit of a relationship with His people, God provided a new and better way—yes, better than the temple. God sent His Son, Christ Jesus, to "tabernacle" among us (see John 1:14). Nowhere was this transition more dramatically pictured than in the temple itself on the day that Christ died. "And Jesus uttered a loud cry, and breathed His last. And the veil of the temple was torn in two from top to bottom." In this dramatic way, God showed the world that He had accepted Jesus's sacrifice for our sin; no more sacrifices were needed in the temple. God illustrated this new plan by allowing people open access to Himself. "We have confidence to enter the holy place by the blood of Jesus, by a new and living way which He inaugurated for us through the veil, that is, His flesh."

To make this access even more intimate, God chooses today to reveal His presence through His Spirit, who lives in every believer. "Do you not know that you are a temple of God and that the Spirit of God dwells in you?" Furthermore, we have the promise that one day we will need no temple at all. The apostle John wrote, "I saw no temple in it [the new Jerusalem], for the Lord God the Almighty and the Lamb are its temple." We will see and dwell with God face-to-face!

See Mark 15:37–38; John 1:14; 1 Corinthians 3:16; Hebrews 10:19–20; and Revelation 21:22.

Jerusalem's Old City walls south of the Jaffa Gate. In the distance once stood the palace of Herod the Great, where Pontius Pilate stayed while in Jerusalem for Passover.

NOW THE *Passover* AND UNLEAVENED BREAD WERE TWO DAYS AWAY; AND THE CHIEF PRIESTS AND THE SCRIBES WERE SEEKING HOW TO *seize* HIM BY STEALTH AND *kill* HIM.

— MARK 14:1

WHAT ARE YOU *Looking* FOR?

S CRIPTURE IS *silent* ABOUT THE EVENTS that happened on the Wednesday of Jesus's final week. However, this midweek mark was far from peaceful. Anticipation, even dread, hung heavily in the air around the Old City.

During this soulful holiday week, everybody was looking for something. The religious were looking to Passover to remember their deliverance from Egypt. Zealots were looking for the revolutionary who would lead them to freedom from Rome. Rome's legions were looking for anyone unruly among the crowds. And every Jew was looking for the Messiah.

Just a few days before, by His choice of entrance into the city, Jesus had made the clear, intentional statement that He was the Messiah. Indeed, the One promised, prophesied, and now here. Yet in spite of the signs, few understood the implications of His announcement, and those few who did, rejected His claim.

The tension must have been thickest in the city streets. Conspiracy. Sharp whispers. Shifting eyes. Enemies in the shadows . . . the talk of blood money. And while the disciples watched their backs, the Pharisees watched for a break in the crowd in order to snare Jesus.

Only Jesus understood the events that would happen that weekend, anticipated before the foundation of the world, foretold by the seers and prophets. In spite of the thousands of opportunities to escape Jerusalem, Jesus set His heart on what would be accomplished there in days to come.

And it would all begin tomorrow.

See Luke 9:51; 19:47; and Revelation 13:8.

Who were people looking for?
"For indeed Jews ask for signs and Greeks search for wisdom;
but we preach Christ crucified, to Jews a stumbling block and to
Gentiles foolishness, but to those who are the called, both Jews
and Greeks, Christ the power of God and the wisdom of God."
(1 Corinthians 1:22–24)

Thursday

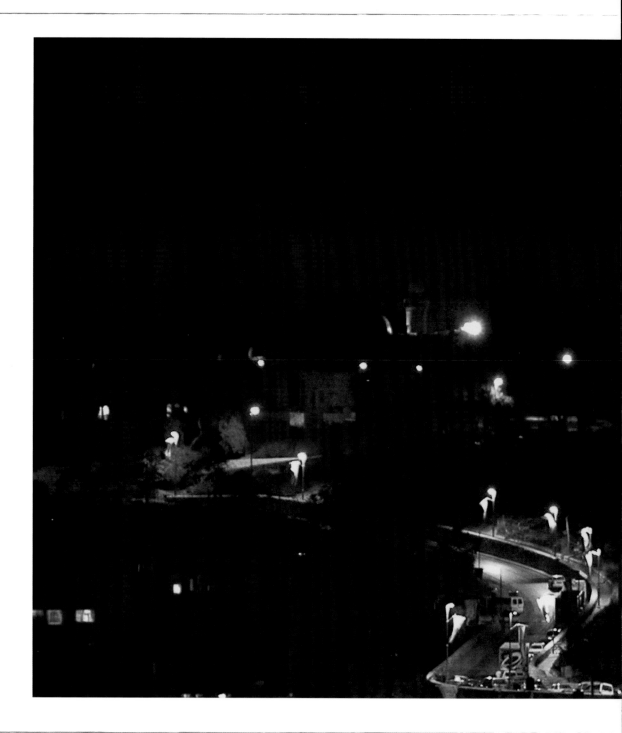

The dome of the Dormition Abbey towers above the western hill of Jerusalem, where Jesus and His disciples ate the Passover in a lamp-lit Upper Room.

The Cenacle, a room rebuilt by Crusaders in the tenth century, stands on the southwestern hill of Jerusalem at the traditional location of the Upper Room where the Last Supper took place.

AND HE SAID TO THEM, "I HAVE EARNESTLY DESIRED TO EAT THIS *Passover* WITH YOU BEFORE I *suffer*; FOR I SAY TO YOU, I SHALL *never* AGAIN EAT IT UNTIL IT IS FULFILLED IN THE *kingdom of God.*"

— LUKE 22:15–16

PICTURE *Jesus* AND HIS DISCIPLES on that Thursday night reclining in a random circle around a low table. They would have faced each other as they ate the ceremonial Passover meal, just as faithful Jews had done for centuries. Since the disciples had been walking with Jesus for three years, they had celebrated three Passovers with Him. But this one was different. They had never heard the message that Jesus gave them on that night, nor did they have any idea how significant their gathering would be.

In accordance with Jewish religious tradition, they would have been quoting from the ancient Scriptures, remembering the days when their forefathers were enslaved in Egypt and delivered by God through His servant Moses. Suddenly, they noticed that Jesus was no longer participating in the conversation. He looked somber—perhaps more somber than He had looked during their three years together.

As they watched with curiosity, Jesus took a piece of unleavened bread and broke it. Then He raised His eyes and prayed. The disciples didn't know it was the last night they would be with Jesus, but He knew.

"Take, eat; this is My body."

What? What was He talking about? They must have looked back and forth at each other questioningly. The Master had never said anything like that before. His words suddenly broke with tradition, and they were completely confused. He told His disoriented disciples to eat the brittle, unleavened bread, reminding them that it was a symbol—a tangible picture—of His body that would soon be given on their behalf.

Imagine the stunned silence. Imagine the questions that swarmed through the minds of the disciples: *Is He really going to die? When? What will happen to us? Will we die too? What about the kingdom He promised? Have all these years with Him been in vain?* Their stomachs were in knots. The Gospels give no indication that a word was spoken in response. For a change, the band of men sat in absolute, total silence.[1]

See Exodus 12; Matthew 26:20–30; Luke 22:14–20; and 1 Corinthians 11:23–26.

This foundational wall of the traditional site of the Last Supper holds a piece of fascinating history. A section of the wall (see large stones at bottom of picture) was part of a first-century synagogue where Jewish Christians worshipped. If the structure had been simply a Jewish synagogue, it would have been physically oriented toward the temple. But the earliest Christians chose to build this synagogue where the Last Supper had occurred and to orient the building in direct line with the Church of the Holy Sepulcher, the traditional site of Jesus's crucifixion, burial, and resurrection.

"Divine Servant" ® is the copyrighted and trademarked creation of Christian artist Max Greiner, Jr., of Kerrville, Texas © (www.maxgreinerart.com)

The powerful moment when Jesus washed Peter's feet is depicted in Max Greiner, Jr.'s sculpture "Divine Servant," located on the campus of Dallas Theological Seminary.

PETER SAID TO HIM, "*Never* SHALL YOU *wash* MY FEET!"
JESUS ANSWERED HIM, "IF I *do not* WASH YOU,
YOU HAVE *no part* WITH ME."

—JOHN 13:8

Proud Hearts AND Dirty Feet

No one really *understood* JUST HOW SIGNIFICANT that seder meal was. No one but Jesus. Jesus knew His "hour had come." He was living in the shadow of the cross, less than eighteen hours away.

He told the disciples, "I have earnestly desired to eat this Passover with you before I suffer." And in the middle of His talk, a dispute—literally a verbal fight—arose among the disciples. They argued over which one of them was regarded as the greatest. How ridiculous for this solemn night! What shameless pride!

The argument was going strong and heavy when all of a sudden the disciples heard water splashing. Without saying a word, the One you would least expect to be doing the lowest servant's duty was kneeling beside Matthew, washing his feet. The cool water ran over his ankles then across and between his toes. Jesus dried Matthew's feet with a soft towel and moved on to the next disciple.

The room was deathly silent. They were willing to fight over the throne, but nobody fought over the towel. Their hearts were proud and their feet were dirty. Jesus had some important truths still to teach them, but He couldn't until they replaced their pride with humility.

When Jesus knelt before Peter to bathe his feet, Peter said to Him, "Never shall You wash my feet!" At first that may sound humble, but his response was actually self-assertive, a form of subtle pride. He pulled his feet back, refusing to humble himself and allow Jesus to be who He really was—a Servant who came to wash the sin of pride from all of them. Pride keeps us from being vulnerable, protects us from being exposed.

So, Jesus answered Peter, "If I do not wash you, you have no part with Me." Connecting the dots, Peter surrendered.

Finally, Jesus put away the towel and bowl, covered His under tunic with His outer garment, and sat down again to eat.

If ever a man had a reason to be proud, Jesus did. He had never once been contaminated by sin. Never once had He failed because of carnality. He came to His last hours in perfect obedience, having accomplished the Father's will. No other human on earth can die with that sense of reality. If there was ever a time to dispatch the angels to display His glory, that would have been the moment. But He didn't. That's what made Him so great, you see. At His most critical hour, He was washing feet.[2]

See Luke 22:14–26 and John 13:5–15.

The Passover table includes the seder plate which contains:
- *A roasted shank bone—a reminder of the Passover lamb.*
- *A roasted egg—a symbol of the festival sacrifice offered in the temple at Jerusalem.*
- *Maror—a bitter herb or horseradish which reminds participants of the Israelites' bitter slavery in Egypt.*
- *Haroset—a mixture of apples, nuts, cinnamon, and wine which represents the mortar the Israelite slaves used in Egypt.*
- *Parsley—dipped into a dish of salt water before being eaten, it symbolizes spring and the renewal of life.*
- *Three matzohs—these pieces of unleavened bread are reminiscent of the manna provided in the wilderness.*
- *Four cups of wine—typifying the fourfold promise of redemption given in Exodus 6:6–7.*
- *Cup of Elijah—usually a tall goblet placed in the center of the table to commemorate the honored guest, Elijah the prophet, who would announce the coming Messiah.*

A gnarled, ancient olive tree in the Garden of Gethsemane

AND HE WENT A LITTLE BEYOND THEM, AND FELL ON HIS FACE AND PRAYED, SAYING, "MY FATHER, IF IT IS POSSIBLE, *let* THIS *cup pass* FROM ME; YET NOT AS I WILL, BUT AS *You will.*"

— MATTHEW 26:39

SOMETIME LATE THAT NIGHT, *Jesus and His men* left the Upper Room and made their way through the streets of Jerusalem. They passed the lower pool and exited out of the city walls through the Fountain Gate. Because the city was bursting with Passover pilgrims camping along the hills and roads, nobody would have noticed this group of men walking down into the Kidron Valley, together for the last time.

Biblical history is buried on the slopes of the Kidron Valley. During the Passion Week, Jesus daily walked the steep path that cut through the valley between the east wall of Jerusalem and the Mount of Olives. It was here that King Asa burned the idol made by his grandmother Maacah (1 Kings 15:13) and King Hezekiah built a tunnel to bring water from the Gihon Spring, saving Jerusalem from the Assyrian siege in 2 Chronicles 32. Here, King Josiah had all the equipment used in Baal worship destroyed (2 Kings 23:4). David crossed the Kidron Valley, barefoot and weeping at the betrayal of his son Absalom (2 Samuel 15:23, 30). The alleged tombs of Jehoshaphat and Zechariah also dot the slope. The upper part of the Kidron is called the "Valley of Jehoshaphat," the valley of "judgment" (Joel 3:2).

Thursday evening was all about last times. The Passover had been their last meal together. For the last time, they were going to their familiar spot on the Mount of Olives. Jesus looked at His friends, fully aware that it was the last time they would be together before they would abandon Him. And that was only a short time away.

Jesus knew that within the next couple of hours He would hear the voices of His captors coming up the hill with torches, slashing the night. He would not run, though He could. They would think they were taking Him by force, but He knew what they could not have known. This was not the march of the condemned but a strategic battle of a war in which victory was promised and assured.

Jesus fought the battle here, in the hour before. In essence, He said, "Let it pass. Let this cup pass." He pleaded with the Father three times in the shadows of the olive trees, in the loneliness of His choice, "Let this cup of suffering pass."

He also won the battle here. Refusing to create the canyon that a stubborn will would have carved, He uttered in essence, "My Father . . . not what I want but what You want." Surrender. Jesus's will and the Father's were one, as it always had been. No distance between them. There would be enough distance the next day. That night, under the gnarled olive trees, He drew close to the Father in prayer.

He had come to do the will of the Father, and so He freely submitted to the Father's plan. In His surrender, He won an important battle on the road to victory.

See Matthew 26:36–46; Mark 14:32–42; and Luke 22:39–46.

Jesus likely climbed these first-century stairs from the valley floor to Caiaphas's house, which is today adjacent to the Church of Saint Peter in Gallicantu on the western hill of Jerusalem.

AND PETER *remembered* THE WORD WHICH JESUS HAD SAID,
"BEFORE A *rooster crows*, YOU WILL *deny* ME THREE TIMES."
AND HE WENT OUT AND *wept* BITTERLY.

—MATTHEW 26:75

TODAY, A PEACEFUL MONASTERY IN *Jerusalem's* SOUTHERN VALLEY offers no clue to the horrific atrocities that occurred near there in the days of Judah's kings. In Jesus's day, the city dump lay in this gorge. Some suggest that fires continually burned the trash, and so Jesus used the smoldering landfill as an illustration of hell's eternal flames.

One has to wonder if this is the reason Judas's desperate regret led him to this ravine known as the Hinnom Valley. For here, according to tradition, the guilt-ridden betrayer of Christ hung himself and then fell headlong, spilling his innards. Hence, the residents later named the place *Hakeldama* or "Field of Blood." On that same day, Peter committed a sin just as wrong as the one Judas had committed, and yet Peter's regret just resulted in a good cry (and a changed life). What made the difference?

An example of first-century silver coins

Like these two disciples, as we come face-to-face with the raw truth of our carnal hearts, our guilt will lead us in one of two directions. As Paul wrote, "For the sorrow that is according to the will of God produces a repentance without regret, leading to salvation, but the sorrow of the world produces death." While Judas's sorrow led him to a needless, desperate act—bowing to sin's penalty—Peter's sorrow led him to grace . . . *to seeking sin's remedy.*

God intends the pangs of shame to lead us away from our guilt and toward His grace. For although sin leads us down into the Hinnom Valley, Jesus offers us the path back out—up to Calvary. With our sins forgiven, we then have no reason to feel shame but every reason to embrace the new life Jesus offers.[3]

See Matthew 26:69–27:14; Acts 1:18–19; and 2 Corinthians 7:10.

The monastery of St. Onuphrius in the Hinnom Valley marks the traditional location of Judas's death.

Friday

The walls of the Citadel on the far western edge of the Old City

Herod the Great's Citadel, Pontius Pilate's residence while in Jerusalem. This is likely where Pilate judged Jesus.

PILATE SAID TO THEM, "THEN *what shall I do* WITH JESUS WHO IS CALLED CHRIST?" THEY ALL SAID, "*Crucify Him!*" AND HE SAID, "WHY, WHAT EVIL HAS HE DONE?" BUT THEY KEPT SHOUTING ALL THE MORE, SAYING, "*Crucify Him!*"

— MATTHEW 27:22–23

Our HISTORICAL PERSPECTIVE *allows* US TO SEE with clarity what many in Jesus's day could not see. But Jesus understood better than anyone that the six trials He endured were a ruse, nothing other than the machinations of corrupt men jealously guarding their power. To make matters worse, they draped their outrageous behavior in the august robes of religious piety. How pathetic they must have appeared before the eyes of Deity.

The religious authorities cast Jesus in the role of villain and accepted the applause — even the admiration — of an undiscerning public. They successfully covered their tracks so that no one realized their impropriety, their lust for power, and their shameful conspiracy to destroy an innocent individual. The Jewish people failed to see the astounding blessings they were forfeiting by killing their Messiah. No one will ever know how God's plan would have unfolded if they had embraced Him.

Very few situations in life are more frustrating than suffering injustice alone and unnoticed. Feelings of outrage demand justice. Bitterness longs for revenge. Hopelessness begs heaven for relief. Loneliness screams to be heard as a watching world stands aloof. During those dark, painful, lonely times, the silence of heaven can be deafening.

If this is presently your experience, rest assured, you are not alone. The Lord sees your suffering, and He will not allow it to go on forever unanswered. He will see justice done, though perhaps not at the time or in the manner you would prefer. Nevertheless, the agony you suffer, though it feels overwhelming, will not go to waste. If you allow it, this experience can be the vehicle by which God delivers His greatest blessings to you.

The trials of Jesus came to a predictable end because they arrived at a foregone conclusion. Jesus was not the kind of Messiah the seditious rabble wanted. Jesus was not the puppet ruler the wealthy and powerful could control. Jesus was not the revolutionary threat Pilate hoped to legitimately condemn. The only matter these habitually contentious parties could agree upon was that the death of Jesus would solve their problems.

"So [Pilate] then handed Him over to them to be crucified."

See Matthew 26:57–27:26; Luke 22:66–23:25; John 18:12–19:16; and 1 Peter 2:23.

The Ecce Homo Arch — meaning literally, "Behold, the Man" (John 19:5) — is the alleged site where Pilate presented a scourged Jesus Christ, bound and crowned with thorns, to a hostile crowd shortly before His crucifixion.

"When Pilate saw that he was accomplishing nothing, but rather that a riot was starting, he took water and washed his hands in front of the crowd, saying, 'I am innocent of this Man's blood; see to that yourselves'" (Matthew 27:24).

THE SIX ILLEGAL TRIALS OF JESUS		
Judge	**Verse**	**Judgment**
Annas	John 18:13–23	Declared guilty of irreverence
Caiaphas	Matthew 26:57–68	Declared guilty of blasphemy
The Sanhedrin	Luke 22:66–71	Declared guilty of blasphemy
Pilate	Luke 23:1–4	Found innocent, overruled by mob
Herod Antipas	Luke 23:8–12	Mistreated and mocked, no decision
Pilate	Matthew 27:15–26	Found innocent, allowed to be crucified

The traditional Via Dolorosa, "the Way of the Suffering" (see route 2 above), marks a faith exercise, not a historical route. To follow the path that the condemned Christ Jesus walked, begin on the west side of the city at the Citadel, Herod the Great's palace (see route 1 above). Pilate usually resided there when he came up from Caesarea to ensure crowd control during the great Jewish feasts; he was most likely there when the Sanhedrin sent Jesus to him at daybreak on Friday (John 19:13).

JESUS . . . WHO FOR THE JOY SET BEFORE HIM *endured* THE CROSS,
DESPISING THE SHAME.

— HEBREWS 12:2

CHRONOLOGY OF EVENTS ²	
Event	**Approximate Time**
Prayer and agony at Gethsemane (Matthew, Mark, Luke)	Late evening
Betrayal by Judas and arrest of Jesus (Mark 14:43–46; John 18:12)	1:30 a.m.
Irregular, unauthorized inquiry at Annas' residence (John 18:13–23)	2:00 a.m.
Unofficial trial at Caiaphas' residence (Matthew 26:57–68; John 18:24)	3:00 a.m.
Formal, official trial before Sanhedrin in their chamber to confirm capital sentence (Mark 15:1; Luke 22:66–71)	6:00 a.m. ("when it was day")
First interrogation by Pilate at official residence (Matthew 27:1–2, 11–14; Luke 23:1–7; John 18:28–38)	6:30 a.m. ("when morning had come . . . and it was early")
Audience/mockery before Herod (Luke 23:8–12)	7:00 a.m.
Final judgment by Pilate (All Gospels)	7:30 a.m.
Scourging in Praetorium (All Gospels)	8:00 a.m.
Nailing of hands and feet to the cross (All Gospels)	9:00 a.m. ("it was the third hour")
Darkness (Matthew, Mark, Luke)	Noon ("when the sixth hour had come, darkness fell")
Death of Jesus (All Gospels)	3:00 p.m. ("and at the ninth hour")
In less than twenty-four hours, Jesus goes from arrest to execution.	

See Matthew 27:27–32; Mark 15:16–20; Luke 23:26–31; and John 19:1–15.

WHAT WAS JESUS *Thinking?*

WHAT THOUGHTS FILLED *Jesus's* MIND IN THE HOURS FROM THE GARDEN OF GETHSEMANE TO THE CROSS?

Never had Jesus felt weaker. More in pain. More human. More alone. But in spite of the hostility and injustice, Jesus kept on entrusting Himself to His Father.

When He stood stripped, oozing, broken, despised in His suffering . . .

When every nerve in His body quivered in agony as they whipped open His flesh . . .

When silent tears spilled down His face . . .

. . . Jesus handed Himself over to His Father for safekeeping.

His Father knew who Jesus was and knew what He was doing and why. His Father judged righteously. (Read 1 Peter 2:23.)

WHAT WAS *Jesus* THINKING AS HE HUNG BETWEEN HEAVEN AND EARTH?

Jesus, almost dead, thought of you. He thought of presenting you to His Father, washed in the blood that now coursed down His side. His thoughts were on the joy ahead.

But Jesus's contemplations were interrupted by the voices from those passing by and from the cross next to His with the temptation: *Save Yourself.*

Satan had tried that strategy before . . . at the beginning of Jesus's ministry. Perhaps he taunted Jesus again now in the end. *Save Yourself!*

But Jesus couldn't save Himself from the cross *and* save us from the penalty of our sin. So He chose His own death . . . and *your* life. He chose you—and it gave Him joy enough to stay on the cross. To endure. To be your Savior. (Read Hebrews 12:2.)

See Isaiah 56:3–4; Luke 4:13; and Philippians 2:6–8.

The ceiling of the Church of the Holy Sepulcher

THEN THEY BROUGHT [JESUS] TO THE PLACE *Golgotha,*

WHICH IS TRANSLATED,

Place of a Skull.

— MARK 15:22

THE *Place* OF A SKULL

The Church of the Holy Sepulcher

THE EARLIEST AND STRONGEST *Christian tradition* places the location of Jesus's crucifixion, burial, and resurrection at a site in Jerusalem that today has no inkling of its original appearance. The Aramaic name of this rocky outcropping, Golgotha (*calvaria* in Latin), reflects death in its translation: "Place of a Skull."

The name of the church built over the site evokes images just as eerie—the Church of the Holy Sepulcher. (*Sepulcher* means a "crypt" or "tomb.") After entering the building today, those accustomed to Western worship may indeed feel aghast: gold drips from icons, chanting fills the spaces, and incense rises among cold stone walls. Six sects of Christendom display jealous rivalries over the goings-on within.

But look past the traditionalism to the tradition of history and you'll find an unbroken connection to the central event of all time. The Jerusalem Christian community held worship services at this site until AD 66, and during the fourth century, Constantine built a church on the site to memorialize the place of Christ's resurrection.

Since that time, the church has been built, rebuilt, and expanded. (Much of what we see today stems from the Crusader period.) Different religions, races, and sects have obscured much of the original site. Yet Christian tradition declares that it is most likely at this place that Christ died and rose again. Ironically, in the very place where the religiously jealous fight over rights, rules, and whose faith is in charge, the need for Christ's death remains clear: *religion couldn't get us to God—we needed our Savior.*

The central shrine of Christendom thus demonstrates the need for the place it hallows.[3]

See Matthew 27:33–56; Mark 15:22–47; Luke 23:33–49; and John 19:17–37.

[JESUS] SAID,
"IT IS *finished!*" AND
HE BOWED HIS HEAD
AND *gave up*
HIS SPIRIT.

— JOHN 19:30

It's a paradox, really. History's darkest day became its brightest. The injustices that pinned Jesus to the tree satisfied, strangely, the justice of God. The sinful activities that caused men to turn against Him proved that they were mere instruments in God's sovereign hand. The cross was the Father's plan for Jesus. Nothing pictures His heart more passionately than the cross of Jesus Christ. Nothing. And while God the Father gave His love, Jesus, God's Son, gave His life.

IN THE FIRST THREE HOURS *on the cross*—with spikes piercing His hands and feet and pus oozing from the raw inflammations on His back—Jesus's only words revealed concern for others. He forgave a criminal dying beside Him, entrusted His mother into John's care, and looked on His murderers with compassion: "Father, forgive them; for they do not know what they are doing."

Their words, however, revealed different hearts. "Let this Christ, the King of Israel, now come down from the cross," the chief priests and the scribes mocked, "so that we may see and believe!" "He saved others; He cannot save Himself," they blasted.

Darkness shrouded Jerusalem during Jesus's final three hours of life. During this time the Gospels record absolutely nothing spoken—until the very end. The darkness reflected the unimaginable spiritual agony Jesus endured.

"My God, My God, why have You forsaken Me?" In that moment, Jesus entered into spiritual death—that is, separation from the Father. Never in all eternity had Jesus endured this incomprehensible severance. But He willingly embraced it, knowing that the penalty for the sins of all humanity received its atonement then and there.

Right there, the new covenant began, the universe was redeemed, and every sin ever committed was paid for.

"It is finished!" Jesus shouted. He raised Himself against the nails to draw a final breath. "Father, into Your hands I commit My spirit." Even in the blur of His pain and in the agony of spiritual death, Jesus entrusted His destiny to the Father's will.

Jesus's body fell limp, motionless, and silent.

In that instant—a mere three hundred yards east—the temple experienced *anything* but silence. A deafening rip filled the courts as the veil that separated humankind from the Holy of Holies tore in two from top to bottom. Like the sky that "tore" open above Jesus's baptism, so the renting of the veil revealed the Father's acceptance of Jesus's death on our behalf. Centuries of sacrifices—burnt offerings wafting their pleasing aroma heavenward—found ultimate fulfillment in the flawless sacrifice of Jesus.[4]

See 1 Samuel 16:7; Mark 11:12–14, 19–22; and Luke 16:15.

JESUS'S SEVEN SAYINGS ON THE CROSS

1. "Father, forgive them; for they do not know what they are doing" (Luke 23:34).

2. "Truly I say to you, today you shall be with Me in Paradise" (Luke 23:43).

3. "Woman, behold, your son! . . . Behold, your mother!" (John 19:26–27).

4. "My God, My God, why have You forsaken Me?" (Matthew 27:46).

5. "I am thirsty" (John 19:28).

6. "It is finished!" (John 19:30).

7. "Father, into Your hands I commit My spirit" (Luke 23:46).

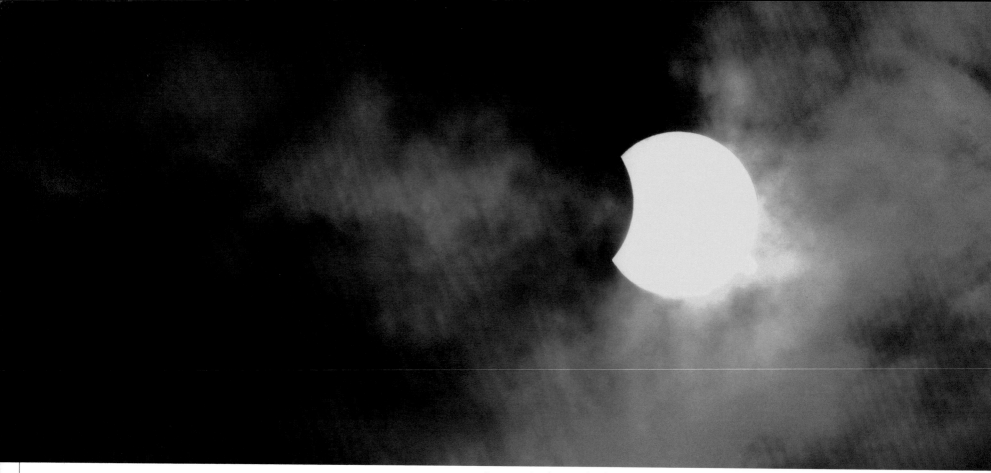

Picture it. It's only 3 p.m., but the "Place of a Skull" is pitch-dark. God, Light Himself, turns away from His Son as He bears the sins of the whole world. And there Jesus hangs, not a soul realizing that it is the most epochal moment in history.

AT THE NINTH HOUR JESUS *cried out* WITH A LOUD VOICE, "ELOI, ELOI, LAMA SABACHTHANI?" WHICH IS TRANSLATED, "MY GOD, *My God,* WHY *have You* FORSAKEN ME?"

—MARK 15:34

WHEN JOSEPH OF ARIMATHEA REQUESTED *Jesus's* body from the cross and laid it in his own new tomb nearby, it was as if all the dreams that surrounded this dead Messiah now lay buried alongside His lifeless corpse. The huge, immovable stone before the entrance seemed to entomb the potential for all future hope. Death felt so unforgiving and final.

Just days prior, Jesus had mounted the foal of a donkey, a recognized symbol of peace and an unmistakable identification with the Messiah, and had ridden into Jerusalem to the cheering of thousands. He was their Messiah. He had promised abundant life. His followers fully expected that He would become their king and that Israel would again be prosperous and free. But now, as the sun fell behind the horizon toward the end of an unforgettable week, the Son of God lay cold and lifeless in a tomb just outside the city walls.

The sorrow that hung over the disciples' hearts felt heavier than the black skies that hovered over Jerusalem. The darkness that began at noon perhaps extended throughout the evening until night consumed it. As the disillusioned disciples cowered in dark corners, they may have wondered if the sun would ever shine again.

As the sun set and the Sabbath began, nothing made sense in light of the prophecies which Jesus had fulfilled, in light of the promises He made, and given the complete confidence they had placed in Him. The people clearly wanted a righteous king, but as He lay dead, the chief priests were busy restocking the Annas Bazaar and Israel's political leaders were seeking ways to exploit Pilate's newfound popularity. Not only had Jesus failed to improve Israel, but the nation's future seemed even bleaker than before.

Discouragement and desperation reigned supreme among Jesus's followers. The Light had gone out of the world.[5]

See Mark 15:43–46; John 19:38–42; 2 Corinthians 5:21; and 1 Peter 2:24; 3:18.

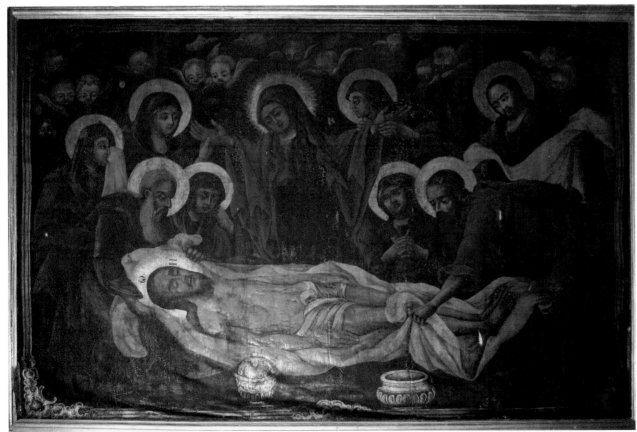

A painting that hangs in the Church of the Holy Sepulcher depicts the preparation of Jesus's body for burial.

Saturday

Early morning light over the Old City

A quiet Sabbath morning in the Old City of Jerusalem

NOW THE WOMEN WHO HAD COME WITH HIM OUT OF GALILEE FOLLOWED, AND SAW THE TOMB AND HOW HIS BODY WAS LAID. THEN THEY RETURNED AND PREPARED SPICES AND PERFUMES. AND ON THE *Sabbath they rested* ACCORDING TO THE COMMANDMENT.

— LUKE 23:55-56

ROOSTERS DON'T *observe* the Sabbath, it turns out.

Peter would have awakened Saturday morning to the loud, repetitive, and humiliating reminder of his denial of Jesus—and of the Savior's piercing gaze. The reality of facing every morning for the rest of his life with a raucous flashback of his failure must have seemed unbearable. Just when Peter thought he could weep no more, the bitter tears must have again flowed down a face wrinkled with regret.

No doubt Saturday dragged long in the thoughts of Jesus's disciples. The Sabbath allowed for no work or considerable activity. It was as if God's Law forced them to sit and to think . . . and to lament their failures. The cross had thrust them into the ugly face of their misplaced hopes for glory.

Jesus would soon show them that the Messiah didn't fail their expectations. Quite the opposite! Their own expectations had failed them. The shattered disciples had built their hopes on their own dreams of glory and greatness and not on what Jesus had told them. Greatness in God's eyes comes through living with a servant's heart—the kind of life Jesus had modeled in His life and in His death. Though they had walked in the footsteps of Jesus for years, they had failed to hear His words. Even being upstairs with Jesus and eating the Passover lamb had failed to open their eyes. It took the cross.

Jesus clearly foretold His death to His men—and it unfolded with all the uncompromising precision He predicted. But His death wasn't all He promised. It was only the beginning.

In creating the world, God ceased working on the Sabbath, or Saturday. That means that God *began* creation on a Sunday morning, the same day of the week Jesus rose from the dead. The next morning as the sun pierced the darkness, Peter's rooster would crow again, announcing a very, very different new day.[1]

See Luke 24:13–27 and John 12:31–33.

This statue of Peter, denying Christ on the evening of His arrest, rests in the courtyard of the Church of Saint Peter in Gallicantu on the western hill. According to tradition, this was the location of the palace of the high priest Caiaphas, where Jesus was taken after His arrest. Gallicantu means "the cock-crow."

EASTER
Sunday

Sunrise over the city of Jerusalem

Easter lilies

"O *death*, WHERE IS YOUR *victory*? O *death*, WHERE IS YOUR *sting*?"

—1 CORINTHIANS 15:55

Resurrection!

I<small>T WAS THE DAWN THAT CHANGED</small> *everything.*

Although that Sunday morning the sun rose over the northeastern edge of Jerusalem just like every other morning before or since, that dawn marked a new day in history. And while that cemetery may have looked like any other Jewish cemetery of its day, it was amazing, holy, resurrection ground.

The plan that God the Father had set in place before the foundation of the world—the plan to rescue humanity from its downward spiral—was fully engaged. In a free fall since that day in the garden when Adam and Eve chose to sin rather than to live with God, we have fumbled in the darkness, at a distance from God. But God's plan was to get us back. And Easter Sunday marks the event that made it all possible.

The sign that everything had changed was when Jesus Christ, Messiah, breathed earth's air again. The promised Savior of the world stood on the other side of the grave. His suffering and death on the cross absorbed God's holy wrath, which had been poured out in full on Jesus, and the righteous debt that sin had created was satisfied. Jesus was the only one who could have paid it, and on that Sunday morning His victory over death proved that His sacrifice had been accepted. Sin no longer held humanity hostage. Death no longer had the last word. *Jesus was alive.*

No doubt on that morning the celebration of all time broke out in heaven as the angels let loose with awestruck hallelujahs. Hell gasped in horror. Ironically, the ones slowest to understand what had happened were the primary recipients of this gift, the greatest act of love the world has ever known.

We're still catching our breath.

See John 20:1–18; Romans 1:4; 5:8; 1 Corinthians 15:55; and 1 Peter 1:23.

"But on the first day of the week, at early dawn, they came to the tomb bringing the spices which they had prepared. And they found the stone rolled away from the tomb, but when they entered, they did not find the body of the Lord Jesus" (Luke 24:1–3).

The Garden Tomb in Jerusalem, while most likely not the tomb of Jesus, still offers a peaceful place to meditate on His resurrection.

BUT PETER GOT UP AND *ran* TO THE TOMB; STOOPING AND LOOKING IN, HE *saw* THE LINEN WRAPPINGS ONLY; AND HE WENT AWAY TO HIS HOME, *marveling* AT WHAT HAD HAPPENED.

—LUKE 24:12

ONLY THOSE WHO HAVE *known* THE WEIGHT of sudden, devastating, intimate grief can understand why Mary was at Jesus's tomb so early that morning. Nothing could have kept her away from that one last loving

duty. Who knows if her tears had been constant since she stood by His cross on Friday afternoon or if the dull pain that numbs every nerve had taken over. Regardless, when she saw the stone rolled from the tomb and Jesus's body missing, she couldn't hold back the sobs. *Where is His body? Must they steal everything?*

Imagine her surprise when a man stood before her and spoke her name in a voice she knew so well, "Mary."

See John 20:11–16.

ONLY THOSE WHO LOVE THE *Lord Jesus* can imagine the joy these friends must have felt when the truth sank in, filling the gaps between the seismic cracks of this weekend. *He's alive.* They had witnessed His body broken, yet they could touch Him, hug Him, see Him again—with nothing but a few scars to remind them of the horror. Last Friday they had heard Him commit His Spirit into the hands of His Father—yet on Sunday there He was, in the flesh—talking, laughing, eating, smiling at them and with them. Life itself had changed in the days since Friday. Everything had been different without Him. Yet there He was, the One they loved. The Sinless One who had died for them. Friend, Rabbi, Teacher, Messiah, Savior. *Alive.* Nothing would be, or could be, the same again. They would spend an eternity rejoicing in what had happened.

Imagine their willingness when a few days later Jesus would say, in effect, "I have a job for you to do until I come again."

See Matthew 28:16–20; Acts 1:8; and 1 Corinthians 15:1–8.

ONLY THOSE WHO HAVE *known* COMPLETE, UNFORGIVEABLE failure could understand the radical grace in the angel's message, "But go, tell His disciples and Peter, 'He is going ahead of you to Galilee; there you will see

Him'" (Mark 16:7). "Make sure Peter knows," the angel at the tomb made a point of communicating. Amazing! The risen Christ wanted Peter to know where to find Him. *Could the Lord have forgotten what Peter could not?*

Imagine the moment Peter's eyes met Jesus's later that day. Imagine the grace in His greeting, "Peace."

See Matthew 26:33–35, 73–75; Mark 16:1–7; and John 20:19–20.

This first-century Roman road was the traditional route to Emmaus, located seven miles from Jerusalem. Jesus's followers would have been traveling this road or one like it when, "while they were talking and discussing, Jesus Himself approached and began traveling with them" (Luke 24:15).

THEY SAID TO ONE ANOTHER, "WERE NOT OUR HEARTS *burning* WITHIN US WHILE HE WAS *speaking* TO US ON THE ROAD, WHILE HE WAS *explaining* THE SCRIPTURES TO US?"

— LUKE 24:32

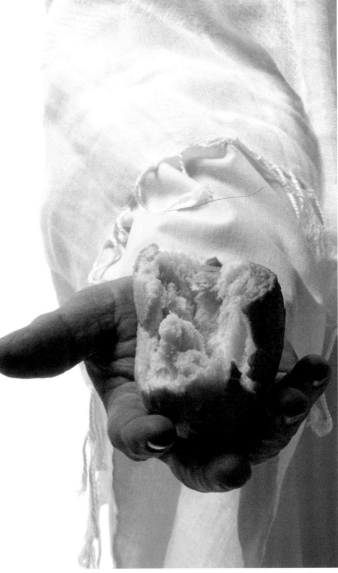

As the *sun rose* on Sunday morning and the Passover feast came to an end, two of Jesus's followers left for home. Discouraged and disillusioned, they resolved to leave their foolish dreams in Jerusalem forever. Even as rumors of resurrection circulated, the dejected pair began the seven-mile walk to the village of Emmaus.

They were conversing about all that had happened. While they were debating, Jesus Himself approached and began to walk with them, "but their eyes were prevented from recognizing Him." He asked them what they talked about so intensely.

"And they stood still, looking sad. One of them, named Cleopas, answered and said to Him, 'Are you the only one visiting Jerusalem and unaware of the things which have happened here in these days?'"

His question was laughable. If anyone understood, it was Jesus! And if anyone was clueless, it was Cleopas! Nevertheless, Jesus played along, "What things?" "The things about Jesus the Nazarene," they replied, "who was a prophet mighty in deed and word in the sight of God and all the people, and how the chief priests and our rulers delivered Him to the sentence of death, and crucified Him. But we were hoping that it was He who was going to redeem Israel."

As they talked and walked along, Jesus peeled away their faulty perspectives one layer at a time until they could see clearly from Scripture how His death and resurrection encompassed the crowning event for the Messiah. They had heard the reports of His resurrection, but they simply refused to believe. If they had believed that Jesus was alive, they would have been walking *toward* Jerusalem, not away. They would have also accepted His trials, crucifixion, and burial as the fulfillment of all He had promised, not the end of all their hopes.

As the afternoon sun sank closer to the horizon, the two disciples were so intrigued with this stranger that they invited Him to stay the night with them in Emmaus. Jesus accepted the offer, while still maintaining His anonymity.

"When He had reclined at the table with them, He took the bread and blessed it, and breaking it, He began giving it to them. Then their eyes were opened [literally, *completely*] and they recognized Him [literally, *fully understood who He was*]; and He vanished from their sight" (Luke 24:30–31).

Can you picture their faces at that moment? They had been with the risen Lord! It was Him all along! "And they got up that very hour and returned to Jerusalem, and found gathered together the eleven . . . saying, 'The Lord has really risen.'" He is risen indeed![1]

See Luke 24:13–35.

"When [Jesus] had reclined at the table with them, He took the bread and blessed it, and breaking it, He began giving it to them. Then their eyes were opened and they recognized Him; and He vanished from their sight" (Luke 24:30–31).

How To *Begin* a Relationship with God

Where do these thoughts about the Passion Week of Jesus Christ find you? You may have heard this story all your life but now realize that you have a responsibility to interact with what you've heard. Here is what you need to know: Jesus Christ Himself said that He came into our world for one purpose — "to seek and to save that which was lost" (Luke 19:10).

There's no question about who He's referring to as "lost." We all are. We're all sinners. If the circumstances of your life have lined up in such a way that today you see that reality — that you need help, that you need a Savior — then there's good news ahead for you. Jesus came "to seek and to save" you. Please read on to understand four truths about this great gift that God has provided and that can be yours for the asking.

Our Spiritual Condition: Totally Depraved

The first truth is rather personal. One look in the mirror of Scripture, and our human condition becomes painfully clear:

> "There is none righteous, not even one;
> There is none who understands,
> There is none who seeks for God;
> All have turned aside, together they have become useless;
> There is none who does good,
> There is not even one." (Romans 3:10–12)

We are all sinners through and through — totally depraved. Now, that doesn't mean we've committed every atrocity known to humankind. We're not as *bad* as we can be, just as *bad off* as we can be. Sin colors all our thoughts, motives, words, and actions.

If you've been around a while, you likely already believe it. Look around. Everything around us bears the smudge marks of our sinful nature. Despite our best efforts to create a perfect world, crime statistics continue to soar, divorce rates keep climbing, and families keep crumbling.

Something has gone terribly wrong in our society and in ourselves — something deadly. Contrary to how the world would repackage it, "me-first" living doesn't equal rugged individuality and freedom; it equals death. As Paul said in his letter to the Romans, "The wages of sin is death" (Romans 6:23) — our spiritual and physical death that comes from God's righteous judgment of our sin, along with all of the emotional and practical effects of this separation that we experience on a daily basis. This brings us to the second marker: God's character.

God's Character: Infinitely Holy

How can God judge us for a sinful state we were born into? Our total depravity is only half the answer. The other half is God's infinite holiness.

The fact that we know things are not as they should be points us to a standard of goodness beyond ourselves. Our sense of injustice in life on this side of eternity implies a perfect standard of justice beyond our reality. That standard and source is God Himself. And God's standard of holiness contrasts starkly with our sinful condition.

Scripture says that "God is Light, and in Him there is no darkness at all" (1 John 1:5). God is absolutely holy — which creates a problem for us. If He is so pure, how can we who are so impure relate to Him?

Perhaps we could try being better people, try to tilt the balance in favor of our good deeds, or seek out methods for self-improvement. Throughout history, people have attempted to live up to God's standard by keeping the Ten Commandments or living by their own code of ethics. Unfortunately, no one can come close to satisfying the demands of God's law. Romans 3:20 says, "By the works of the Law no flesh will be justified in His sight; for through the Law comes the knowledge of sin."

Our Need: A Substitute

So here we are, sinners by nature and sinners by choice, trying to pull ourselves up by our own bootstraps to attain a relationship with our holy Creator. But every time we try, we fall flat on our faces. We can't live a good enough life to make up for our sin, because God's standard isn't "good enough" — it's *perfection*. And we can't make amends for the offense our sin has created without dying for it.

Who can get us out of this mess?

If someone could live perfectly, honoring God's law, and would bear sin's death penalty for us—in our place—then we would be saved from our predicament. But is there such a person? Thankfully, yes!

Meet your substitute—*Jesus Christ*. He is the One who took death's place for you!

> [God] made [Jesus Christ] who knew no sin to be sin on our behalf, so that we might become the righteousness of God in Him. (2 Corinthians 5:21)

GOD'S PROVISION: A SAVIOR

God rescued us by sending His Son, Jesus, to die on the cross for our sins (1 John 4:9–10). Jesus was fully human and fully divine (John 1:1, 18), a truth that ensures His understanding of our weaknesses, His power to forgive, and His ability to bridge the gap between God and us (Romans 5:6–11). In short, we are "justified as a gift by His grace through the redemption which is in Christ Jesus" (Romans 3:24). Two words in this verse bear further explanation: *justified* and *redemption*.

Justification is God's act of mercy, in which He declares righteous the believing sinners while we are still in our sinning state. Justification doesn't mean that God *makes* us righteous, so that we never sin again, rather that He *declares* us righteous—much like a judge pardons a guilty criminal. Because Jesus took our sin upon Himself and suffered our judgment on the cross, God forgives our debt and proclaims us PARDONED.

Redemption is Christ's act of paying the complete price to release us from sin's bondage. God sent His Son to bear His wrath for all of our sins—past, present, and future (Romans 3:24–26; 2 Corinthians 5:21). In humble obedience, Christ willingly endured the shame of the cross for our sake (Mark 10:45; Romans 5:6–8; Philippians 2:8). Christ's death satisfied God's righteous demands. He no longer holds our sins against us, because His own Son paid the penalty for them. We are freed from the slave market of sin, never to be enslaved again!

PLACING YOUR FAITH IN CHRIST

These four truths describe how God has provided a way to Himself through Jesus Christ. Because the price has been paid in full by God, we must respond to His free gift of eternal life in total faith and confidence in Him to save us. We must step forward into the relationship with God that He has prepared for us—not by doing good works or by being a good person, but by coming to Him just as we are and accepting His justification and redemption by faith.

> For by grace you have been saved through faith; and that not of yourselves, it is the gift of God; not as a result of works, so that no one may boast. (Ephesians 2:8–9)

We accept God's gift of salvation simply by placing our faith in Christ alone for the forgiveness of our sins. Would you like to enter a relationship with your Creator by trusting in Christ as your Savior? If so, here's a simple prayer you can use to express your faith:

> *Dear God,*
>
> *I know that my sin has put a barrier between You and me. Thank You for sending Your Son, Jesus, to die in my place. I trust in Jesus alone to forgive my sins, and I accept His gift of eternal life. I ask Jesus to be my personal Savior and the Lord of my life. Thank You. In Jesus's name, amen.*

If you've prayed this prayer or one like it and you wish to find out more about knowing God and His plan for you in the Bible, contact us at Insight for Living. Our contact information is on the following pages.

If you desire to find out more about knowing God and His plan for you in the Bible, contact us. Insight for Living provides staff pastors who are available for free written correspondence or phone consultation. These seminary-trained and seasoned counselors have years of experience and are well-qualified guides for your spiritual journey.

Please feel welcome to contact your regional Pastoral Ministries by using the information below:

United States
Insight for Living
Pastoral Ministries
Post Office Box 269000
Plano, Texas 75026-9000
USA
972-473-5097,
(Monday through Friday,
8:00 a.m. – 5:00 p.m. Central time)
www.insight.org/contactapastor

Canada
Insight for Living Canada
Pastoral Ministries
Post Office Box 2510
Vancouver, BC V6B 3W7
CANADA
1-800-663-7639
info@insightforliving.ca

Australia, New Zealand, and South Pacific
Insight for Living Australia
Pastoral Care
Post Office Box 443
Boronia, VIC 3155
AUSTRALIA
1 300 467 444
www.insight.asn.au

United Kingdom and Europe
Insight for Living United Kingdom
Pastoral Care
PO Box 553
Dorking
RH4 9EU
UNITED KINGDOM
0800 915 9364
+44 (0)1306 640156
pastoralcare@insightforliving.org.uk

If you would like to order additional copies of *Sunday to Sunday: A Pictorial Journey Through the Passion Week* or order other Insight for Living resources, please contact the office that serves you.

United States
Insight for Living
Post Office Box 269000
Plano, Texas 75026-9000
USA
1-800-772-8888
(Monday through Friday,
7:00 a.m. – 7:00 p.m. Central
time)
www.insight.org
www.insightworld.org

Canada
Insight for Living Canada
Post Office Box 2510
Vancouver, BC V6B 3W7
CANADA
1-800-663-7639
www.insightforliving.ca

Australia, New Zealand, and South Pacific
Insight for Living Australia
Post Office Box 443
Boronia, VIC 3155
AUSTRALIA
1 300 467 444
www.insight.asn.au

United Kingdom and Europe
Insight for Living United Kingdom
PO Box 553
Dorking
RH4 9EU
UNITED KINGDOM
0800 915 9364
www.insightforliving.org.uk

Other International Locations
International constituents may contact the U.S. office through our Web site (www.insightworld.org), mail queries, or by calling +1-972-473-5136.

PALM SUNDAY

1. Harold W. Hoehner, *Chronological Aspects of the Life of Christ* (Grand Rapids: Zondervan, 1977), 138.

2. Portions of this devotional are excerpted from Wayne Stiles, *Walking in the Footsteps of Jesus: A Journey through the Lands and Lessons of Christ* (Ventura, Calif.: Regal, 2008), 115–17.

3. W. E. Vine, *An Expository Dictionary of New Testament Words with Their Precise Meanings for English Readers*, vol. 4 (Old Tappan, N.J.: Fleming H. Revell, 1966), 206.

4. Vine, *An Expository Dictionary of New Testament Words*, 206.

MONDAY

1. Adapted from Wayne Stiles, *Walking in the Footsteps of Jesus: A Journey through the Lands and Lessons of Christ* (Ventura, Calif.: Regal, 2008), 123.

TUESDAY

1. Adapted from Charles R. Swindoll, *Jesus: The Greatest Life of All* (Nashville: Thomas Nelson, 2008), 162, 167–68.

THURSDAY

1. Adapted from Charles R. Swindoll, *The Darkness and the Dawn: Empowered by the Tragedy and Triumph of the Cross* (Nashville: Word, 2001), 20–23.

2. Adapted from Charles R. Swindoll, "Humility Personified," in *Following Christ . . . the Man of God*, message series (1975).

3. Adapted from Wayne Stiles, *Going Places with God: A Devotional Journey through the Lands of the Bible* (Ventura, Calif.: Regal, 2006), 80.

FRIDAY

1. Adapted from Charles R. Swindoll, *Jesus: The Greatest Life of All* (Nashville: Thomas Nelson, 2008), 200.

2. Chart adapted from Charles R. Swindoll, *The Darkness and the Dawn: Empowered by the Tragedy and Triumph of the Cross* (Nashville: Word, 2001), 340.

3. Adapted from Wayne Stiles, *Going Places with God: A Devotional Journey through the Lands of the Bible* (Ventura, Calif.: Regal, 2006), 82.

4. Adapted from Wayne Stiles, *Walking in the Footsteps of Jesus: A Journey through the Lands and Lessons of Christ* (Ventura, Calif.: Regal, 2008), 155–56.

5. Stiles, *Walking in the Footsteps of Jesus*, 157.

SATURDAY

1. Adapted from Wayne Stiles, *Walking in the Footsteps of Jesus: A Journey through the Lands and Lessons of Christ* (Ventura, Calif.: Regal, 2008), 157–58.

EASTER SUNDAY

1. Adapted from Charles R. Swindoll, "Encountering Jesus along Life's Road" in *Jesus: The Greatest Life of All*, message series (1999).

Copyrights

Sunday to Sunday: A Pictorial Journey Through the Passion Week

From the Bible-Teaching Ministry of Charles R. Swindoll

Charles R. Swindoll has devoted his life to the clear, practical teaching and application of God's Word and His grace. A pastor at heart, Chuck has served as senior pastor to congregations in Texas, Massachusetts, and California. He currently pastors Stonebriar Community Church in Frisco, Texas, but Chuck's listening audience extends far beyond a local church body. As a leading program in Christian broadcasting, *Insight for Living* airs in major Christian radio markets around the world, reaching people groups in languages they can understand. Chuck's extensive writing ministry has also served the body of Christ worldwide and his leadership as president and now chancellor of Dallas Theological Seminary has helped prepare and equip a new generation for ministry. Chuck and Cynthia, his partner in life and ministry, have four grown children and ten grandchildren.

Published By:

IFL Publishing House
A Division of Insight for Living
Post Office Box 251007
Plano, Texas 75025-1007

Editor in Chief: Cynthia Swindoll, President, Insight for Living
Executive Vice President: Wayne Stiles, Th.M., D.Min., Dallas Theological Seminary
Writer: Barb Peil, M.A., Christian Education, Dallas Theological Seminary
Theological Editor: Derrick G. Jeter, Th.M., Dallas Theological Seminary
Content Editor: Amy L. Snedaker, B.A., English, Rhodes College
Copy Editors: Jim Craft, M.A., English, Mississippi College
  Kathryn Merritt, M.A., English, Hardin-Simmons University
Project Coordinator, Creative Ministries: Melanie Munnell, M.A., Humanities, The University of Texas at Dallas
Project Coordinator, Communications: Sarah Magnoni, A.A.S., University of Wisconsin
Proofreader: Paula McCoy, B.A., English, Texas A&M University-Commerce
Designer: Steven M. Tomlin, Embry-Riddle Aeronautical University, 1992–1995
Production Artist: Nancy Gustine, B.F.A., Advertising Art, University of North Texas
Photos:
  Todd Bolen for BiblePlaces.com: cover, pages 2, 3, 6, 16, 17, 24–26, 28–30, 33, 35–39, 43–48, 50, 62–63, 66, 68
  Daniel Frese for BiblePlaces.com: pages 3, 58–59
  Wayne Stiles: cover, pages 1, 3, 4–5, 9, 10, 27, 31, 52, 53, 57, 61
  Barb Peil: pages 7, 8, 9, 11, 18, 19, 31, 39
  IFL Staff: page 40
  Image of "Hill of Golgotha" by Maltings Partnership, page 32: copyright © 2008 by Crossway, a ministry of Good News Publishers. All rights reserved worldwide. Used by permission.

An effort has been made to locate sources and obtain permission where necessary for the quotations used in this passport. In the event of any unintentional omission, a modification will gladly be incorporated in future printings.

ISBN: 978-1-57972-874-8

Printed in the United States of America